INDIE AUTHOR MAGAZINE

HELLO AND WEL-COME!

I'm Indie Annie, and I'm thrilled you're reading this gorgeous full-color version of IAM. Did you know that you can also access all the information, education, and inspiration in our app? It's available on both the iOS App Store and Google Play. And for those that prefer to listen to me read articles, you can pop over to Spotify or our website. Happy Reading!

X

IndieAuthorMagazine.com

FORMATS

INDIE AUTHOR MAGAZINE

Volume 2 • Issue 2 • February 2022

This Issue's Featured Author: INES JOHNSON

FORMATS

NFT Books: A Work in Progress

Devil in the Details— Medical Mixups

10 Tips for Facebook

Make Some Noise: What—and How— Indie Authors Gain From a Growing Audiobook Industry

ON THE COVER

INDiE
AUTHOR MAGAZINE

PUBLISHER
Chelle Honiker

CREATIVE DIRECTOR
Alice Briggs

CONSULTING EDITOR
Nicole Schroeder

COPY EDITOR
Lisa Thompson

WRITERS
Angela Archer
Elaine Bateman
Patricia Carr
Bradley Charbonneau
Laurel Decher
Fatima Fayez
Gill Fernley
Greg Fishbone
Remy Flagg
Chrishaun Keller Hanna
Jac Harmon

WRITERS
Marion Hermannsen
Kasia Lasinska
Bre Lockhart
Anne Lown
Sìne Màiri MacDougall
Merri Maywether
Lasairiona McMaster
Susan Odev
Nicole Schroeder
Emilia Zeeland

PUBLISHER
Athenia Creative
6820 Apus Dr.
Sparks, NV, 89436 USA
775.298.1925

ISSN 2768-7880 (online)–ISSN 2768-7872 (print)

Get documents done anywhere

Now available for your Android & iOS mobile device

Dragon® Anywhere professional-grade mobile dictation makes it easy to create documents of any length, edit, format and share them directly from your mobile device-whether visiting clients, a job site, or your local coffee shop.

- ✓ Continuous dictation and no word limits
- ✓ 99% accurate with powerful voice editing and formatting
- ✓ Access customized words and auto-text across all devices
- ✓ Share documents by email, Dropbox, Evernote and more

Select a flexible pricing plan **Subscribe now** ▾   *Credit Card Required. After your 7 day free trial, the monthly subscription begins at $15 per month. Cancel at anytime.

WriteLink.To/Dragon

From the Publisher

THE PRODUCT OF PERSEVERANCE

When it comes down to a hero's journey, the one thing that makes the story compelling is their ability to overcome the obstacle. What odds did they beat? What was previously insurmountable that they have now conquered? And, more importantly, how did they achieve success?

GRIT. DETERMINATION. STICK-TO-IT-NESS.

The answer, more often than not, comes down to one thing. They simply kept going.

Now that the warm fuzzy glow of the new year has passed and the resolutions are broken (a statistical probability, I'm afraid) it's time to dig out the only weapon in our arsenal that can redeem those ambitious goals you set for 2022, back when you were full of hope and optimism.

PERSEVERANCE.

You can't edit a blank page. *Write some words.* You can't market what you haven't finished. *Quit scrolling social media.* You missed a deadline. *Set a new one.*

Don't start over. Keep going. Pretend that you never stopped. Don't wait for another milestone day of the week or month to give yourself a fresh start. **Start again where you are right now.**

You're the hero. It's your journey. Only you can write your way out of this obstacle. Give yourself the same gift of perseverance that you'd give one of your fictional friends.

Make your life and career unputdownable.

To your success,
Chelle
Publisher
Indie Author Magazine

Dear Indie Annie,

I recently completed my first book and sent it to an editor. I got the first round of edits back, and it sounds like another person wrote my book! How do I keep my editor from strangling my voice?

Strangled in Strasburg

DEAR STRANGLED,

Or can I call you by the name of the place in which you reside? Strasburg is a beautiful city, and Strangled? Well, it's a tad melodramatic, if you don't mind me saying so.

That's not to say that I don't understand how you feel, dear darling Strasburg. Oh, I do.

It is a special alchemy finding the right editor. They may be very good at their job but might not be the best fit for you. I need to ask you, how did you find them? Did you ask them to edit a sample piece of your work? Do they edit other writers in your genre? What is their background/experience?

This is your first book and receiving an extensive edit of your much-beloved baby is difficult for us all, even after years of successful writing. It's even harder with your first child.

And our books are our children. I liken it to looking for a suitable nanny. Many who apply for the role will be qualified, but you have to find the one that best fits your family, your needs, and your ethos.

Sometimes the nanny will need to challenge your parenting skills. Sometimes they will have to be firm with your cherubic offspring. But you need to trust that their actions come from a place of truly understanding what you are trying to achieve.

Are you looking for Mary Poppins, Nanny McPhee, or Jo Frost from Supernanny? I will admit all three personalities scare the living daylights out of me, but that doesn't mean I shouldn't listen to their advice.

All advice, including editing, is simply that—advice. It is your choice whether

Need help from your favorite Indie Aunt?
Ask Dear Indie Annie a question at
IndieAnnie@indieauthormagazine.com

you take it or leave it. You say they have reworded so much of your original, you don't recognize it as yours anymore. It sounds to me like the editor has been a tad overzealous and forgotten their role, which is to nudge your manuscript toward a better version of the original, not to create their own masterpiece.

If I were you, I would ask myself, "Do the suggested changes improve the original?" Some of the edits may be grammatical or style changes to help the manuscript flow more smoothly so that the reader can understand you more clearly. If so, analyze what they are doing. Can you improve on any negative patterns? I once had a strong love of ellipses… I … really loved … my drama dots. It took a long time to break the habit, but my editor was right. My writing improved tenfold by becoming aware of my bad habits and breaking them.

At first, though, I railed against this observation because … well, that was my voice.

It wasn't though. My voice was sassy, humorous, and fast-paced. The beloved ellipses slowed down my writing, made it predictable and lazy.

So, before you dismiss your editor's comments, look for patterns, themes, and areas for improvement that they have observed and consider if they have a point. That doesn't mean you have to wholesale accept everything they say. Maybe they are right about that split infinitive or Oxford comma, but it could be a style choice and not how you wish to write.

It's easy to get lost in your story and not see the gaping holes that someone with fresh eyes will notice. This is why many authors use beta readers. They should be readers in your genre who will let you know honestly if your story has issues.

Get another set of eyes on your work, perhaps even with the editor's comments attached, so that you can get an honest appraisal of what is going on. If, after all this self-reflection, you still believe that the editor's suggestions do not suit your voice, then, my dear Strasburg, it is time to say thank you and move on.

You wouldn't keep a nanny who tried to strangle your children. Remember, you are the client. You are in charge. Ultimately, it is your decision.

Happy writing,
Indie Annie

10 TIPS FOR
FACEBOOK

Facebook can be a great place for authors to meet and get to know other authors and readers. It's easy to post and to add a variety of information to your posts, including emoticons, photos, and videos, how you're feeling and what you're doing, check-ins, and more to give people an idea of who you are and what you're interested in.

But of course, what we all want to know is how can we sell our books with our Facebook page? The thing is, apart from paid ads, using Facebook is a bit like going to a series of networking events. You wouldn't (hopefully!) walk into a networking event and immediately start saying, "Buy my stuff, buy my stuff," and it's the same on Facebook too. It really is about being social and building relationships.

So how can you sell your books the right way on your Facebook page?

1 AUTHOR PAGE OR SERIES PAGE?

First, you have a decision to make.

You can set up a page for every book and every series you're going to write, but that's a lot of work. It's easier to simply set up a page for you as an author and share all your books and series under that pen name from there. Though, of course, it is up to you.

The main exception to just having an author page is if you ever write something like Harry Potter or Twilight that's a complete phenomenon. If that happens, you're probably going to need a series page so fans who know the books but don't necessarily know your author name can still get their fix of series news, latest releases, and so on.

2 FILL IN ALL THE THINGS

Fill in as much info as you can everywhere Facebook will let you. Use your bio and your About section to give people a sense of who you are, what they can expect, and what genre(s) you write in. Use keywords so people can search for you, such as thriller writer or sweet romance author.

Add your other social links and include a link to your author website. Here, you could link to the main home page, you could send people to a landing page to sign up to your newsletter, or you could even send them straight to your Amazon author page.

You can also connect your page to Instagram, share posts on both platforms, and create Instagram ads. To do this, click the 'Manage' button to go to your professional dashboard and choose 'Linked Accounts'. From your dashboard, you can also click on 'Podcasts' and link to your podcast if you have one.

The more information you provide, the easier it is for fans to find you and find your books.

Pro tip: Preview your page as a reader would see it. Click on the three dots on the right of your page and click 'View As' to make sure it looks how you want it to look.

3 WHAT TO POST

There's no need to struggle for something to post. Here are just some ideas that can keep you going:

Share blog posts from your website, share other authors' blog posts, do a cover reveal, share unedited snippets from your latest WIP, and give sneak peeks and teasers from your upcoming release. You can talk about your writing process, share funny typos and autocorrects, talk about your pets, share a photo of your writing space, or ask readers to name a character or a place in your next book. You can look for ARC readers, share your other social links, talk about books you're reading, ask questions about readers' favorite books and characters, and talk about what gave you the idea for your book. You can share any events you're doing, like author signings; do a short live reading of part of your next book; and talk about what you do outside of writing.

Pro tip: Make it easy on yourself and use relevant hashtags so readers can easily find you. Use your genre hashtags, your book title, and series title. Also try more general hashtags, like #amwriting, #WriterWednesday, and #SampleSunday.

4 BE AUTHENTIC

In addition to the mega list above, always, always be yourself. It's much less work than trying to be someone you're not, and readers can tell if you aren't being true to yourself. Genuine passion and enthusiasm are appealing, engaging, and contagious, and people will connect with you far more easily if you really mean what you're saying.

(5) BE CONSISTENT

The worst thing you can do on Facebook is to post all day every day for a few weeks and then stop. If tumbleweeds have taken over your Facebook page and you need to sweep off the cobwebs before you can even see where to click to make a new post, that doesn't give readers the best impression, especially ones who are new to you. Try to post at least a couple of times a week, preferably a couple of times a day so that they always have something new to see and to engage with. Empty pages don't sell books, but genuine, personable, and relevant consistent posts build relationships that can lead to book sales over time.

(6) BUILD RELATIONSHIPS WITH READERS

As we mentioned earlier, don't be one of those whose entire Facebook page consists of "here's my new book" or "buy my book." Get to know your readers and let them get to know you. Raving superfans aren't born from a string of ads; they're born from genuine exchanges of views and being able to relate to each other. Also, Facebook loves engagement and replying to your readers' comments isn't only lovely for them, but Facebook will love you too and reward you with increased visibility. We know we don't have to spell it out, but here it is: More visibility means readers can more easily find you and your books.

(7) BUILD RELATIONSHIPS WITH OTHER AUTHORS

Other authors aren't your competition. Billions of readers are out there—more than enough for everyone. Share other authors' new releases on your page, talk about books you really enjoyed, and tag their authors. Being generous does come back to you. You'll find most authors are thrilled to get a shout-out on your page, and many will return the favor when you have a new release. Many other authors also have a group where they'll let you post about your new releases or even do a takeover to introduce you to their readers. You might also find yourself perfectly placed to join an anthology another author is putting together or to take part in a cross-promotion event they're running, which will also expose you to new audiences. Even better, you'll make some fantastic friends and learn a whole lot, which is priceless. As with any kind of networking, give first without expectations, be genuine, and reap the rewards.

8 IMAGES AND BRANDING

Imagine a shop front with a tatty, faded sign, dirty windows, and handwritten notices advertising the goods inside. Now picture a different store with gleaming windows, inviting window displays, and a fresh, consistent look inside and outside. You know which one you're shopping at and so do your readers. Keep all your social media pages, not just Facebook, consistent with your author brand. Use the same fonts, colors, and look everywhere you post and create branded images using Canva, BookBrush, or similar so readers can instantly recognize one of your posts over any other authors' posts.

You'll stand out if you do it right and—you guessed it—so will your books.

9 REGULARLY CHECK YOUR PAGE

With any type of marketing, you will need to step back and look at what you've got every now and again. Perhaps do it when you set your goals for the next year or make a plan to check your Facebook page once a quarter to see if it's still aiming for and reaching the right audience and that your author branding looks as it should. If not, tidy it up, refresh it, and get it back on track.

10 FACEBOOK ADS

We couldn't mention Facebook and not mention how successful Facebook ads can be for book promotion. You need your Facebook page in order to run Facebook ads, so it's worth setting it up for that alone. Check out Mark Dawson's Ads for Authors course when it opens or Bryan Cohen's free 5-Day Author Ad Profit Challenge to learn how to make the most of Facebook ads for selling your books. ■

Gill Fernley

Ines Johnson

STORYTELLING ...
BUT ADD A LITTLE SPICE

This year, Ines Johnson will have written and published over one hundred books. A seasoned author and introvert who loves sticky notes and colorful pens, she's a treasure trove of experience. She's also quick to point out that her processes may not work for everyone.

"Just because Ines said it, don't you follow her. Understand that Ines is Romance forward. Kissing books are what she's looking at, and if it's not that, then I'm not paying attention." Ines says of herself.

And Ines does write kissing books of all flavors: Paranormal, Urban Fantasy, Contemporary, and Erotic. She's admittedly a very specific consumer of stories who prefers her books with a heavy dose of love and doesn't see herself writing outside of various romantic subgenres, but one thing is clear: Great advice can often be applied universally.

THE STORYTELLER AND THE FORMULA

As the daughter of a funk musician, Ines grew up with music as the background to her life. She learned that storytelling was present in songs, in everything. "Life is just made up of all these parts, and you can

> As the daughter of a funk musician, Ines grew up with music as the background to her life. She learned that storytelling was present in songs, in everything.

pick them apart and put them back together in interesting ways …. As a kid watching cartoons, I would be thinking about that, thinking about the structure of things."

She worked in television before writing full-time, just one more avenue where she got to watch stories develop and hone her skills. On that evolutionary path, she became more well versed in story structure and plotting. She applauds the idea of the "obligatory scenes" and says, "People talk about plotting and plots and outlines and beats like it's a bad thing … I hear people sometimes talk about this as 'oh my gosh, that's not creative. You're just following a formula, or you're following a pattern,' and I've never understood that, and I still don't because there's comfort in that repetition. But try to twist that in a different and interesting way."

Along with understanding storytelling, she doesn't shy away from tropes and market research. She knows the trends. She knows the reader expectations. She wants her readers to come away from her stories with a sense of contentment.

"Those patterns are there for a reason, and I think they should be respected. If you are making a cake, you don't all the sudden put in a cup of salt instead of a cup of sugar … maybe even cayenne, you add a kick of it. You add to it, but I think you should not subtract from it because when you subtract, people get uncomfortable, and they're left unsatisfied."

If her journey to bestselling author is any indicator, her readers are definitely satisfied.

NOT-SO-SOCIAL MEDIA

For those reading who don't love being online all the time, Ines is honest about her lack of desire to interact on

the various platforms, preferring to focus on new stories for her readers rather than the social aspect of social media.

Arguably, some of her advice that we can all heed is, "I really pay attention to my strengths, and I go full force with my strengths. I don't really put a lot of time into what I know I'm not good at."

However, introverts can find social places that work for them, and for Ines, that all comes back to storytelling. "I can tell a story with a Facebook ad. I'm telling stories about my characters in my news-letter. I try to use that to my advantage. I like TikTok, but it's only because I'm telling a story. I'm not talking about me. I'm talking about what my characters did, what my characters said. That's interesting, and it's fun for me."

And she is finding success on platforms like TikTok where she can stay character-focused instead of Ines-focused, where she doesn't have to share what she had for dinner or the state of traffic in her neigh-borhood. The takeaway here is that if you don't enjoy something, don't force it. Find the author places you like to be and make the most of them. As Ines says, play to your strengths.

ZERO-SUM PLANNER

While we spoke, it was nearly impos-sible not to notice the artwork that deco-rated Ines's walls. Not abstract colors or figure drawings like you might picture, but whiteboards, calendars, lists, and an impressive number of sticky notes. Ines is a tracker, a planner. She checks her sales daily and knows when sales are generated from a specific source. But she doesn't let tracking take center stage.

"I love to take a colored pen and record the data of my sales every day ... but if you ask me at the end of the day or the next day how many sales I had, I couldn't tell you because I'm not interested in that. I'm interested in the achievement."

Ines knows where her sales are coming from and uses that data to motivate her further, but she doesn't swim in the minutia of it. This approach feels very doable and less overwhelming, like so many pebbles of wisdom she shared.

For those looking to up their planning game, along with Becca Syme's courses that we've talked about in previous articles, Ines also recommends Sarra Cannon's YouTube channel and courses.

FUTURE FOCUSED

If you are wondering what an author with a triple-digit backlist focuses on, the answer for Ines for 2022 would be translations. "I compared my audio sales and my translation sales, and translations by far were killin' it."

Part of her universal advice is that authors should be doing their research. Know what genres are selling in what foreign language markets to make sure you are putting your time and money into the right things for your books. Cowboy Romance might miss the target in Japan, but Urban Fantasy might be a bullseye.

As far as her additional future plans, she said, "I really want to try some simultaneous releases, meaning where I release the e-book, the audiobook, and the print book, including the hardback, all at the same time." She even talked about co-writing and collaborations, followed by the deep breath of a woman with a lot of irons in the fire.

> Know what genres are selling in what foreign language markets to make sure you are putting your time and money into the right things for your books.

The overall impression of author Ines Johnson is one of relatability. She's smart and genuine, focused but friendly. When she talked about having too many story ideas but too little time to write them, the global author collective nodded along at their desks. As the interview ended, I couldn't help but think that this was a human I would happily sit and have a coffee with just to pick her brain for even longer. As a bonus, she had great book recommendations!

To see what Ines is up to, you can join her newsletters on her websites https://InesWrites.com and https://ShanaeJohnson.com but true to her word, she's not very active on social media. Feel free to check out her #booktok videos on TikTok and watch for her sessions at upcoming author conferences in various locations across the US. ■

Bre Lockhart

Hardbacks Made Easy

YOUR STEP-BY-STEP GUIDE TO DECIDING WHICH HARDCOVER OPTIONS ARE RIGHT FOR YOU

Have you ever dreamed of a hardcover edition of your book with a paper jacket, the author bio, and professional photo? Maybe you've played with the idea of a ribbon bookmark or endpapers with a map of your story world. The great news is that hardcovers are possible with print-on-demand, including Amazon's hardcover option, which launched in 2021. Similar to paperback, your costs for hardcover are the creation of cover files and an upload fee plus the usual percentages off the retail price to cover distribution.

WHY CONSIDER HARDCOVER?

Bragging rights alone are a solid reason for hardcover editions. A hardcover omnibus—the print equivalent of a digital box set—would look impressive on your next Zoom call. Hardcovers are perfect for libraries and schools, a crowdfunding campaign (how about a limited edition?), gifts for die-hard fans, direct sales from your website, and for creating a three-fold offer of e-book, paperback, and hardcover to make the e-book pricing look especially appealing.

WHAT ARE YOUR OPTIONS?

Trim sizes, page count and other limiting factors—who can do what for you?

1. **Is your formatted manuscript over 550 pages? Over 800 pages? Or under 75 pages?** A large omnibus, huge novel, or nonfiction title might only work with IngramSpark because of the high page count. Depending on the paper

type and print quality you choose, IngramSpark can produce black-and-white or standard color hardcovers with a maximum of 1200 pages and a premium color hardcover with a maximum of 840 pages. The maximums are lower for tolino (882 pages), Barnes & Noble (800 pages), and Lulu (800 pages). KDP allows a maximum of 550 pages. A slim picture book might only work with IngramSpark or Barnes & Noble, which both have an 18-page minimum. The minimums are higher for Lulu (24 pages), tolino (52 pages), and KDP (75 pages).

2. **Do you want to sell special editions from your website?** Lulu.com or Aerio, available in the US market only, might be your doorway into direct-print sales.

3. **Do you avoid exclusivity clauses?** All these services allow you to distribute your print books with other services.

4. **Do you want a dust jacket?** Only IngramSpark, Lulu, or Barnes & Noble offer that option.

5. **Do you want to lower your shipping costs?** IngramSpark's groundwood paper is reputed to produce a lighter book for the same page count.

Deciding on the trim size, or the dimensions of the finished book, and the type of binding is next. Case laminate has no dust jacket, and the cover design is printed directly on the cover. It's popular for school and library use. Digital cloth or linen wrap are plain or printed hardcovers with dust jackets. See a comparison of available print-on-demand trim sizes for hardcover books offered by Barnes & Noble, KDP, IngramSpark, and Lulu.com below:

Available Print-On-Demand Trim Sizes

IngramSpark	KDP Hardcover	Barnes & Noble	Lulu.com
5 x 8" (203 x 127 mm) ** 5.5 x 8.5" (216 x 140 mm) ** 5.83 x 8.27" (210 x 148 mm) 6 x 9" (229 x 152 mm) ** 6.14 x 9.21" (234 x 156 mm) ** 6.69 x 9.61" (244 x 170 mm) 7 x 10" (254 x 178 mm) 7.5 x 9.25" (235 x 191 mm) 8 x 8" (203 x 203 mm) 8 x 10" (254 x 203 mm) 8 x 10.88" (276 x 203 mm) 8.25 x 10.75" (273 x 210 mm) 8.5 x 8.5" (216 x 216 mm) 8.5 x 11" (280 X 216 mm)	5.5 x 8.5" (13.97 x 21.59 cm) 6 x 9" (15.24 x 22.86 cm) 6.14 x 9.21" (15.6 x 23.39 cm) 7 x 10" (17.78 x 25.4 cm) 8.25 x 11" (20.96 x 27.94 cm)	5 x 8" ** 5.5 x 8.5" ** 6 x 9" ** 6.14 x 9.21" ** 7 x 10" 7.5 x 9.25" 8 x 8" 8 x 10" 8.5 x 8.5" 8.5 x 11" 11 x 8.5" (premium color only, white 70 lb.)	**Digest** ** 5.5 x 8.5" / 140 x 216 mm **A5** 5.83 x 8.27" / 148 x 210 mm **US Trade** ** (6 x 9" / 152 x 229 mm) **Royal** ** (6.14 x 9.21" / 156 x 234 mm)

*Note: Case laminate trim sizes. ** Indicates dust jacket available. Trim sizes listed under Lulu.com allow for global distribution.*

HOW MUCH DO HARDCOVERS COST?

Many factors determine the printing cost for a print-on-demand book: trim size (the dimensions of the finished book), page count, paper type, embossing, jacket or no jacket, ribbon bookmark, and glued or curved stitched spine.

Changing the trim size can change your page count and the printing cost per book or even determine if a project is possible. For example, an omnibus with three novels of 300 pages each comes to 900 pages. That's over the maximum page count for several services. Only IngramSpark can print a book with that page count.

It's worth considering a different trim size. If each of those novels were formatted for 6 x 9 inch trim size, the omnibus could be one size bigger. The Royal Octave (Lulu) is 6.14 x 9.21 inches. With a larger trim size, the page count dropped to 752 pages without a tiny font or tight line spacing, rendering the book unreadable. You will have to reformat your interior file to fit the new trim size, but it might be worth the trouble.

In addition to printing costs, some print-on-demand services have setup fees or charge a percentage to cover their distribution costs. The table on the next page gives you an idea of the costs by provider, but to figure your exact costs, use the cost calculators available on the providers' websites. As the order size increases, the price per unit drops.

Price comparison for a 300-page, 6 x 9 inch hardcover with black-and-white printing on cream paper and a matte cover priced at $29.99 in the US market

Provider	Case Laminate (or Ingram's Textured Digital Cloth)	Jacketed Case Laminate (or Ingram's Digital Cloth)
IngramSpark	$9.76 print charge + setup fee; $3.74 royalty (55% discount)	$11.55 print charge + setup fee; $1.95 royalty (55% discount)
KDP	$9.10 print charge; $8.89 royalty	N/A
Barnes & Noble	$8.84 print charge; $7.65 royalty	$10.17 print charge; $6.32 royalty
Lulu	$15.20 print charge, but a price of $29.99 gives you negative royalties because of Lulu's percentage. Minimum price is $30.40.	$18.80 print charge, but $29.99 gives you negative royalties because of Lulu's percentage. Minimum price is $37.60.
tolino (€29.99 for A5 trim size)	Print charge not stated; €4.93 author royalty **Note:** Setup fee of €14.90 includes ISBN and listing in VLB, paperback and hardcover, non-exclusive contract*.	N/A

WHAT DO YOU NEED TO CREATE HARDCOVERS?

The main difference in setting up hardcover versus paperback editions is the cover file and the dust jacket file, if you want one. If the book's trim size is the same, you can use the same interior file for both the paperback and hardcover editions. It's two for the price of one.

Cover files are unique to each provider. If you create hardcovers on both Amazon and IngramSpark, you will need two different cover files because the thickness of the spine differs slightly for the same page count. Barnes & Noble uses Ingram to print, but Barnes & Noble requires a different ISBN, so the barcode has to be changed on the cover.

Cover and dust jacket templates are available online. Here are a few more helpful tips for your cover design: IngramSpark recommends that any type smaller than 20 point be black only. Cover files should use a CMYK color profile, not RGB. Interior and cover files should be saved in a print-quality PDF format with embedded fonts. Ingram reports that blue will often print as purple. Metallic colors are not recommended.

Now that you have your classy hardcover, use it to your advantage. Offer one gorgeous hardcover as a prize for a giveaway. Add the title information to your ISBN record on Bowker (or Nielsen or whichever agency administers ISBNs in your country). Set sail in the data streams, and help people find your intellectual property in its new clothes. Make a splash. ◼

Laurel Decher

RESOURCES

Cost calculators

1. IngramSpark calculators: https://myaccount.ingramspark.com/Portal/Tools/PubCompCalculator

This calculator shows print charge by country.

Print-and-ship calculator: https://myaccount.ingramspark.com/Portal/Tools/ShippingCalculator

This calculator includes the shipping by country.

2. KDP calculator: https://kdp.amazon.com/en_US/help/topic/GSQF43YAMUPFTMSP

3. Barnes & Noble calculator: https://press.barnesandnoble.com/make-more-money

4. Lulu.com pricing calculator: https://lulu.com/pricing

5. Tolino calculator: Create a free account to see the dashboard and compare prices. The setup fee of €14.90 per print book includes an ISBN and registration with Germany's Books in Print equivalent: Verzeichnis lieferbarer Bücher. This is a great deal for indie authors because registration is normally a €69 minimum that allows for the registration of up to nineteen titles plus an annual fee of approximately €2, according to tolino's website.

6. BoD price calculator: https://bod.de/autoren/buch-veroeffentlichen/preiskalkulation.html

BoD charges €19 per year or €249 per year per book. If the price is on the cover and you want to change the price, that counts as a new edition and costs €249. Or if you have BoD Classic, you pay €19 and release a new edition. They offer ribbon bookmarks, colored endpapers, and curved, stitched spines.

Hardcover trim sizes

KDP: https://kdp.amazon.com/en_US/help/topic/ GVBQ3CMEQW3W2VL6#trimsize

IngramSpark: https://ingramspark.com/plan-your-book/print/trim-sizes and https://ingramspark.com/hubfs/downloads/trim-sizes.pdf

Barnes & Noble: https://help.barnesandnoble.com/app/answers/ detail/a_id/4047/~/b%26n-press%3A-available-trim-sizes-and-paper-stock

Lulu: https://assets.lulu.com/media/guides/en/lulu-book-creation-guide.pdf

Only those trim sizes with global distribution included. If you sell from your website, you may have more trim sizes available to you.

Cover file creation tools

KDP: https://kdp.amazon.com/en_US/help/topic/GDTKFJPNQCBTMRV6

Cover templates:

KDP: https://kdp.amazon.com/en_US/cover-calculator

IngramSpark: https://myaccount.ingramspark.com/Portal/Tools/ CoverTemplateGenerator

Enter your book information, and the template will be emailed to you.

Barnes & Noble: https://press.barnesandnoble.com/book-cover-template-generator

Note: Barnes & Noble has a downloadable template for dust jackets. Since they use Ingram for printing, you can get a template here.

Barcode generators: bookow.com or KDP will generate one for you automatically on upload. IngramSpark's template includes one, but you have to get it from the PDF template in your graphic design software. Bookow.com will create a hardcover template but not a dust jacket template.

Sell books from your website

IngramSpark (US market only):

https://aer.io/

Lulu: Lulu might be a solid option for direct sales via API, Shopify, the new WooCommerce beta, or for bulk sales because they don't charge the distribution fee.

https://lulu.com/lulu-direct

Make Some Noise

WHAT—AND HOW—INDIE AUTHORS GAIN FROM A GROWING AUDIOBOOK INDUSTRY

Sometimes the best books are the ones we don't read.

That's not necessarily referring to those books we leave languishing in our to-be-read piles though those deserve plenty of love and recognition as well. No, there's just something nostalgic about having a story told to you rather than reading it yourself. Perhaps it's the memories of hearing bedtime stories while drifting off to sleep or sitting cross-legged on a scratchy carpet for read-aloud time in grade school. Or maybe it's simply remembering learning to read as a mentor's voice helped you sound out the trickier words.

Of course, nowadays, as adults struggle to fit reading time into their day-to-day lives, many people are trading in their paperbacks for earbuds for an entirely different reason. Amid commutes around town, multitasking at home, hectic schedules, and ever-growing to-do lists, it's no surprise that an estimated one in five Americans, according to a study published in 2021 by Pew Research Center, opt to listen to audiobooks—the paperback's more portable, accessible sibling.

In recent years, both audiobooks and podcasts have seen an uptick in listenership. According to Axios, consumption of spoken-word media has increased by 40 percent in the US since 2014. And in 2021, IBIS-World reported the audiobook industry was worth $1.1 billion. For the independent author, the audiobook industry offers plenty of opportunities to reach more diverse audiences and create another revenue stream—but it can be an expensive investment to start, and just like anything, it's important to consider all your options beforehand.

Beyond the rapid growth of the industry as a whole, audiobooks can provide independent authors with a direct—and sometimes lucrative—additional source of income.

WHY TRY AUDIOBOOKS?

Beyond the rapid growth of the industry as a whole, audiobooks can provide independent authors with a direct—and sometimes lucrative—additional source of income. Depending on your choice in narrator and whether you opt to pay per hour of finished recording or provide a royalty share, audiobooks can be an additional money-maker with little additional effort once you've recouped the cost of production. And even with the industry's steady growth in recent years, audiobooks still yield less competition than e-books, which translates to a greater ability to get noticed and inch upward on bestseller charts, according to the Alliance of Independent Authors.

"What I do is a business," says author Pamela M. Kelley, who has published about a dozen audiobooks, all but one of those in the past two years. "My product is my books, and my customers want audio." Kelley doesn't listen to audiobooks herself, but she says she was convinced to give the format a chance when, at a local book club she attended, she learned that eleven out of the twelve women there said they preferred audio over print. Now, she says her readers have come to expect the option, asking far in advance of new releases whether an audiobook will be published then too.

But audiobooks don't only help their authors. Joshua Berkov, an author and collections management librarian at the North Carolina Library for the Blind and Physically Handicapped, has published three novels and one short story as audiobooks. In his work, he sees "firsthand" the benefit audiobooks can have for people who cannot read print books or e-books, which can be the case for many people with visual impairments, dyslexia, visual processing disorders, or other disabilities.

"My audiobooks are not profitable, but for me, it was all about access," he writes. "I wanted to make sure my books were accessible to people with visual impairments. This was more important to me than whether I might ever make a profit on them."

Berkov's difficulty earning a profit from audiobooks isn't rare. Creating audiobooks can require a hefty upfront cost of either time or money, and like with anything in the independent publishing business, they're not guaranteed to make that investment back in short order. Kelley recommends doing research into other books in your genre to see if audiobooks are in demand from those readers and focusing on newer releases rather than something deep in your backlist as you consider whether to pursue the format.

HOW TO GET STARTED

In spite of the less predictable aspects regarding profit, Kelley emphasizes the ease of production as one advantage to audiobooks. "It's ten thousand times easier than I imagined it," she says. "I think people are so intimidated by it. It seems complicated. It's ridiculously easy. The narrator does all the work."

For each of Kelley's audiobooks, she opted to hire a narrator, paying per finished hour. Berkov also hired his narrators, finding both of them through ACX, an audiobook creation and distribution marketplace run by Amazon. Although Kelley chose to reach out to one of her narrators directly, many authors, such as Berkov, audition interested voice actors with a selection of scenes or dialogue

Audiobooks have a benefit for people who cannot read print books or e-books, which can be the case for many people with visual impairments, dyslexia, visual processing disorders, or other disabilities.

from several characters in the manuscript to find the right fit. If going this route, try to wait a few days before making any decisions on who to hire, Berkov writes, as sometimes the later entrants have taken more care with their auditions.

After that, it's up to the voice actor—the author's only job is to provide notes regarding words that might be mispronounced and to review the narrator's work for any sections you'd like them to re-record. Berkov encourages authors to be honest with their narrators about whether they want them to redo a section or deliver a line differently. "It's your work ultimately, and you deserve to have it sound the way you want it to," he writes.

Narrators generally charge between $250 and $400 per finished hour, with more experienced narrators sometimes costing more, according to Kelley. With one finished hour spanning nine thousand to ten thousand words on average, that means a complete audiobook can cost more than one thousand dollars to create. Alternatively, authors can pay narrators via royalty share, but that comes with its own limitations, such as required Audible exclusivity and a 50 percent split of any royalties with your narrator for seven years.

Authors who are willing to sacrifice their time to save money on audiobook creation have a third option. Author M. L. Buchman records his own audiobooks and has published *Narrate and Record Your Own Audiobook: A Simplified Guide* to help other authors do the same. The process can be arduous—each finished hour of audio can take five to ten hours to record, edit, and produce, according to Independent Book Review—but for authors who have a clear speaking voice and want to save money, the trade-off can be worth it.

Once the audiobook is created, all that's left is to decide on distributors. ACX makes books available through Audible, Amazon, and iTunes, offering a 40 percent royalty for those who agree to an exclusive contract with the marketplace. However, indie authors who pay their narrators per finished hour and who publish wide can sign a nonexclusive contract instead. This provides royalties of only 25 percent from ACX but allows for distribution on other sites, such as Findaway Voices or OverDrive, both popular audiobook distributors that also make books available at libraries.

Authors interested in producing audio-books certainly have a wealth of options, and with the expense associated with the format, Kelley says it's probably best to research what has worked for other authors and to wait until e-book sales are strong for a better chance of earning back your initial investment. When it comes down to it, there's no one-size-fits-all approach to the format—the best way to learn what your readers want might just be to sit back and listen. ■

Nicole Schroeder

NFT Books:
A Work in Progress

A VISION FROM WITHIN THE INFANCY OF CRYPTO PUBLISHING

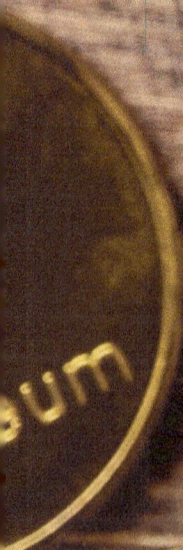

WHAT ARE NFT BOOKS?

I can't tell you for sure. Not yet. What I can do is speculate on what NFT books might become.

The scenarios described in this article are realistic expectations based on existing technologies and the work being done to create the infrastructure of tomorrow. But since the NFT world is evolving quickly, even this forward-looking snapshot may seem quaint and dated soon after this article is published.

IMAGINE THE NEAR FUTURE

It's a beautiful day in the metaverse. There's crypto in your wallet, and your favorite author has just dropped a new book. So you strap on your goggles and enter the virtual world. Or maybe you open your web browser, old school. Or maybe you visit a brick-and-mortar store and tap your phone against an NFT spot on the shelf.

However you choose to travel, there you are.

IMAGINE THE MARKETPLACE

There are many marketplaces, but you've always liked the vibe of Milton's NFT Book Emporium, a mom-and-pop shop with hand-curated lists in a style that matches your aesthetic. Most other marketplaces are web- and metaverse-only, but Milton's sprang from a brick-and-mortar shop in Australia. Or was it Ireland? Either way, those thousand miles of land and ocean between you and that store can be bridged instantly by a VR headset.

Milton's hosts events. They have a book club. They have a cat that wanders with you from room to room, at least in the metaverse rendition of the shop. The website has the same cat in its logo. When you click on the cat, it bats your cursor around the screen.

The marketplace at Milton's uses a cryptocurrency common to many small meta-bookshops, the $BAXTER, named after a famous shop cat. The $BAXTER is specific to books, issued by a DAO that's controlled by book lovers. You like spending $BAXTERs because they're more energy-efficient and

Glossary

DAO - Decentralized Autonomous Organization
https://ethereum.org/en/dao

NFT - Nonfungible Token
https://youtu.be/NNQLJcJEzv0

eco-friendly than crypto coins typically favored by collectors. Plus, the use of $BAXTERs funds a microloan program for booksellers in developing economies, a legal defense pool that assists authors in copyright and contract disputes worldwide, and an anti-censorship advocacy group.

The virtual shelves at Milton's are stocked with NFT books, which are digital files of text or voice narration governed by a smart contract and wrapped into a non-fungible token on a decentralized ledger. You chuckle to yourself at that definition, which sounded like gibberish to you when you first heard it but has since become a way of life.

IMAGINE A SECONDARY MARKET

As long as you're in the marketplace already, you take the opportunity to prune your personal library of some of the NFT books you've already read. Your personal library is linked to your crypto wallet, so it's always as near as your computer, tablet, phone, or headset. And as long as you keep your seed phrase protected, those NFT books are more secure than the physical books in your home.

Milton's will buy your NFT book for an appropriately discounted cash-now price or will list it for you at market value. In fact, many of the books you see on Milton's shelves are second-hand listings that are identical to newly minted NFT books. Some are books that you yourself are currently offering for resale. Your NFT books can exist on a shelf at Milton's or on a dozen

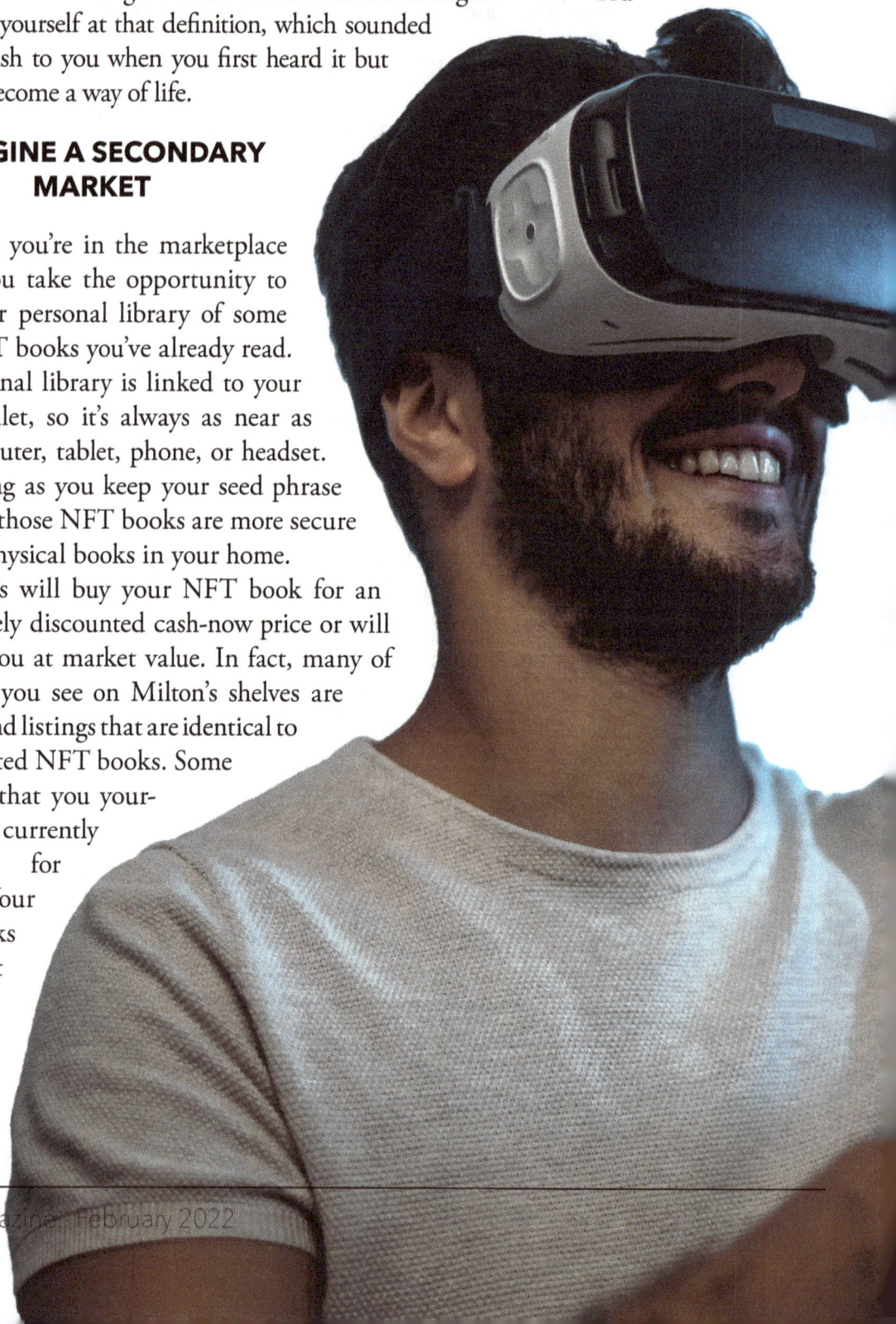

other marketplace shelves and still remain available in your personal library until you accept an offer to sell.

Fortunately for the authors, these NFT books are programmed for secondary royalties. Every time the NFT books are sold, and no matter how many times they're resold, the author instantly receives another royalty payment from the transaction. This, you muse, is one of the major advantages that authors receive from publishing their books as NFTs.

IMAGINE BOOK PIRACY THWARTED

While browsing at Milton's, you chat with the staff, fellow customers, and volunteers who have been designated as moderators of the conversation. You chat for quite a while with a group of enthusiasts from around the world who share your excitement for the new release you came in for.

One of the mods opens a private chat. Along with your interest in the new book, she has taken note of your various roles. You earned one during the early days of the store's metaverse presence. You earned another for saying

nice things about the store on social media. You earned a third for being a frequent customer. "You don't have to buy this book," the mod tells you. "I have a Gold Edition for you."

The Gold Edition of this book is notoriously rare, which makes you suspect that this one might be pirated or forged. But since this is an NFT book, you can check prior transactions back to their source with a few mouse clicks. In moments, like a jeweler peering at a diamond through a loupe, you verify the authenticity of the Gold Edition and let the mod drop it into your wallet.

This is one book you won't be listing for resale. Not for all the $BAXTERs in the world!

IMAGINE SPECIAL EDITIONS AND FEATURES

Your Gold Edition NFT book includes a short-story prequel and an alternate cover. That's fairly standard. But the smart contract that defines the NFT book can perform other feats of magic. Text can update over time, possibly in response to a reader's input or preferences. Holders of one book can automatically receive a copy of the next. A random book holder may be selected as a sweepstakes winner.

You've heard of a mystery writer whose NFT book vanishes page by page as the book is read. A thriller writer who sets her NFT books to self-destruct if they're not completed before a ticking clock counts down. A fantasy author who grants a license for NFT holders to create and publish fanfic while the author receives an automatic royalty. A science fiction author who sells NFTs that allows readers to bring their original characters into his own future books.

Launch events for your favorite author's new book include a special VIP party with a special ticket of admission: a Gold Edition NFT book. When you connect your crypto wallet to the online space, a bot checks whether you have a Gold Edition NFT book on your bookshelf. If you do, a newly granted role unlocks a voice chat with the author and a back-channel text chat for participants. A famous DJ is hosting the afterparty.

You receive a Proof of Participation token at the end of the night. This NFT goes into a gallery of experiences that you can display alongside your bookshelf as if the book itself weren't already enough to make your friends insanely jealous.

IMAGINE THE READING EXPERIENCE

For a moment, you reflect on how the NFT book reading experience has evolved.

In 2021, some NFT books could be read as text files within the marketplace where they were sold. Others linked to a password-protected web page where they could be read with nicer formatting. A handful of experimental releases offered a slicker experience with formatting and page turns that resembled contemporary e-books.

In 2022, everything changed with the mainstreaming of NFT book-specific platforms. These could connect to a crypto wallet, verify ownership, and grant access to an enhanced e-book, audiobook, video clips, or even the ability to print and ship a copy of the physical book. By the end of the year, NFT books had become everything e-books, audiobooks, and physical books had ever been plus a whole lot more.

The $BAXTER launched in 2023, making it easier for Milton's and other metaverse retailers to proliferate, and bringing authors and readers to an NFT book utopia.

OR MAYBE NOT?

This vision depicts just one possible future for NFT books, the marketplaces through which they will be sold, the currencies that will govern their transactions, the platforms that will provide reader experiences, and the organizations that will define crypto publishing for decades to come.

The real future of NFT books is still being written.

SO WHAT ARE NFT BOOKS?

As authors, we can advocate for the future we'd most like to be a part of. Get involved. Learn. Experiment.

NFT books can be anything you want them to be. ■

Greg Fishbone

Tech Tools

Courtesy of IndieAuthorTools.com
Got a tool you love and want to share with us?
Submit a tool at IndieAuthorTools.com

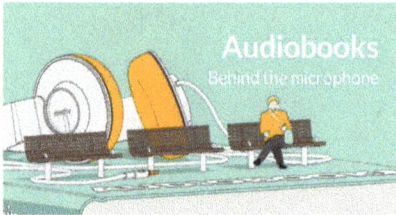

A CLASS BY REEDSY

Behind the Microphone: How to Create a Great Audiobook

Reedsy, the swiss-army knife of usefulness for indies, expands its Reedsy Learning channel with a free 10-day email course taught by audiobook expert David Markowitz. The comprehensive course breaks down the costs and process of audiobook production, as well as tips from his over 25-year career.
https://blog.reedsy.com/learning/courses/publishing/create-great-audiobook

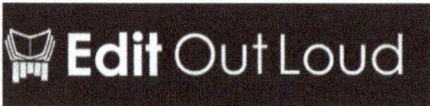

EDIT OUT LOUD

A mobile app to make editing fast and simple.

Upload your novel to this simple mobile app and listen from your smartphone. Tap if you notice something you want to change and a note is made. Another key feature is a tool to find beta readers. Free.

https://editoutloud.com

INKARNATE

If you were the kid that stared at maps of Narnia and Middle Earth and now write books set in your own make-believe world, Inkarnate is for you. Create your own maps with detail, color, and rich assets. Free plans, with their premium annual plan just $25.
https://inkarnate.com

KINGSUMO

Often the hype doesn't match reality when it comes to services that promise "lead generation" but in this case, as with most products produced by the AppSumo team, it does. KingSumo makes it dead simple to grow your mailing list through giveaways, and the best part is they manage all the complex technology. Just choose your prize, configure a few settings, and watch the leads roll in.
https://appsumo.8odi.net/5b17go

MILANOTE

Much like Notion, Evernote, or Google Keep, Milanote organizes clips, images, notes and other data into boards. Comes with templates for creatives and features a clean interface with lots of satisfied users. Free.
https://milanote.com

Getting a Grip on Your Author Platform by Thinking Like a Spider

I f you want to sell books, don't wait and hope that people will magically find you among 4.54 billion internet users. You need a way to cut through the noise, grab their attention, and generate sales.

People talk about having an author platform, but it can feel like an abstract concept. The internet tells you to have your own website, your own email newsletter, a social media presence, a lead magnet, a guest post, launch promos, advertising, and oh-so-many other things. It feels overwhelming. Where do you start? What do you focus on?

Basically, your author platform is everything that you do both online and off-line to help readers find you. What and how you say it is about your author brand—but that's a topic for another day.

If you can understand what your author platform is and how all the pieces fit together, you can more effectively target and strategize your marketing efforts instead of running willy-nilly promos, posting here and there, or only occasionally sending an email to your subscribers.

The best way to wrap your head around this concept is through an analogy. Think of your author platform like a spider's web (you're the spider—but a very nice one), and all the internet users are like flies, zooming around the internet looking for interesting places to land.

The center of your web is your website: your central hub from which all other strands hang. You not only live there, but you also want your visitors to end up there. There, they can find out more about you and sign up for your email newsletter. All your books, your social media links, your blog—if you have one—are all listed there.

But don't bother having a website if you're not going to somehow drive traffic to it. You need to remember that people consume content differently, and different types of content achieve different results. Here, we'll focus on the free stuff—paid advertising is another ballgame.

Imagine that each spoke of your web is a different marketing channel. Social media networks like Facebook, YouTube, your email newsletter, a blog, paid ads, and press releases are all different channels from which you can attract attention.

Let's take Facebook, for example. Generally speaking, photos tend to get more likes, whereas inspirational quotes, memes, and videos tend to get more shares. You need a willingness to test different types of content and learn what your audience responds to. But when you understand what makes them comment, click, or share and when you stop expecting one post to get all three (likes, shares, and comments), you can use it to your advantage as part of your strategy.

Just as the spider creates spokes, it also weaves between the spokes to make the web even stronger. Therefore, to build a stronger platform, you should cross-promote your other channels. From your email newsletter, you can direct fans to your preferred social media network and vice versa. According to We Are Social's 2020 digital report, there are currently 3.8 billion active social media users, and of those users, each person actively uses at least one other social media platform a day and 6.7 different social platforms every month.

What this means for us is that you have plenty of opportunities to reach readers. If you're not sure

- **Social media for building brand awareness**
- **Paid ads for fast-track growth and sales**
- **Email newsletters for deepening relationships**

which platform to focus on, the reality is that it doesn't matter. When you start to grow from focusing on one platform and create cross-channels, your audience will probably follow.

It also means that readers have more touch points to come into contact with you. Some industry professionals focus on signing up people for your email list because you own and control it. However, different people consume content differently. So even though they may not subscribe to your email list, you still have the opportunity to reach them through social channels, or vice versa.

The use of social media and blogging is typically referred to as content marketing or inbound marketing. Using content marketing as a strategy is a long-term, slow-burn effort that makes it hard to track a tangible effect on sales. People won't necessarily indicate that they saw your social media post two days before they bought your book. It's a kind of invisible marketing, but it can contribute to a reader's buying decision.

Blogging is also a great, risk-free method for readers to find you. The reader views this as a "risk-free" method because they don't have to make a large commitment or give away their email address to sign up for your email newsletter.

Blogs offer a free way to build awareness of your brand, but blogging isn't for everyone. If you're just starting out with little or no audience, you might decide to start blogging. Not only does it help you develop your brand voice and style, but it also keeps you writing, attracts new readers, and brings others back to your website. It's also easy to set up, and you can invite your blog followers to sign up for a newsletter later down the line. To maximize the value of having a blog, be sure to add a call to action at the end of your blog posts, such as asking readers to share the blog post on social media or follow you on Facebook.

One of the main spokes of your web will be your email newsletter. This is because it is yours. You control it, for the most part anyway, aside from issues with spam folders and email deliverability. Essentially, you have direct access to a person's inbox—and to someone who liked you enough to trust you with their email address.

The job of your email newsletter isn't strictly about selling them your next book. In the age of personalization, focus on deepening your relationship with those readers. You've moved them from casual browsers to people who know, like, and trust you. Offer value in those emails. That doesn't mean giving them free stories.

We're in the business of providing entertainment, so entertain them, and give them a reason to open your email.

Marketers are moving away from focusing on email open rates, but let's say on average, a good email open rate is around 20 percent. If your open rate is less, try working on your subject lines and header text to increase that. If you're above 20 percent, then that's awesome—keep doing your thing.

Keeping the math basic, even if you're getting the average open rate of 20 percent, 80 percent of your list have still not seen your email. Don't be afraid to resend it. Try a different subject headline, and even if you another 20 percent of people open it, 60 percent still have not seen your email.

By driving people to other places in your web, you have more chances to connect with them. It doesn't feel like a major thing if they don't open your email or they unsubscribe because you can catch them on a social network. If they stop using social media, it's okay because they've signed up for your email list. By having multiple spider web spokes—multiple channels, multiple touch points—you have more opportunities to stay connected with your audience. Your aim is to give readers meaningful ways to connect with you—and by meaningful, we mean meaningful to them.

Like social media, your author platform is a tool to build brand awareness and ultimately drive sales, so how you use it is up to you. Starting out, you may only have two or three spokes (your website, newsletter, Facebook) in your web, which is fine. Building a solid foundation takes time. Don't look at authors with a huge backlist and a marketing budget to match and think you have to immediately do the same. If you're further down the line, then look at which other channels you can use to cross-promote and strengthen your web.

Invite your newsletter readers to like or follow you on social media, and invite your social media followers to sign up for your newsletter. You'll then have a solid author platform to build from.

Angela Archer

Podcasts We Love

Audiobook Speakeasy

Hosted by Rich Miller, The Audiobook Speakeasy podcast is one-to-one chats with audiobook professionals and listeners about all things related to audiobooks. You'll hear from narrators, narration coaches, engineers, editors, audiobook publishing company representatives, casting directors, and power listeners.

https://www.richvoiceproductions.com/audiobook-speakeasy

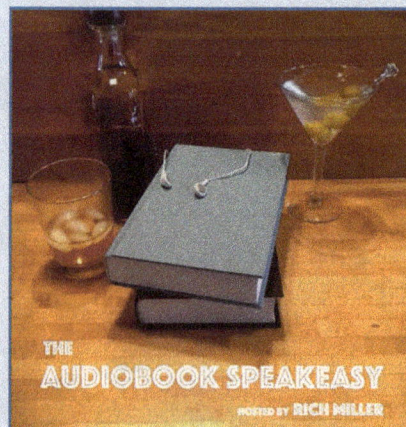

Creator Economics

A podcast hosted by two of the most notorious characters in Digital media:

Reed Duchscher, CEO of Night Media and talent manager of noteworthy creators such as MrBeast, Typical Gamer, and Preston.

Blake Robbins, VC at Ludlow Ventures and the man that helped make 100 Thieves what it is today.

Reed and Blake are on a mission to inform the masses of the success of digital creators, as well as giving a behind-the-scenes look into how such success was possible.

https://podcasts.apple.com/us/podcast/creator-economics/id1534098122

Dreamer Comics Podcast

Every week on the Dreamer Comics Podcast, Omar Spahi interviews a different comic book creator every week to teach you how to make your own comics from start to finish. They dive deep into what to do to get your comic book created, published and sold to fans.

https://dreamercomics.libsyn.com

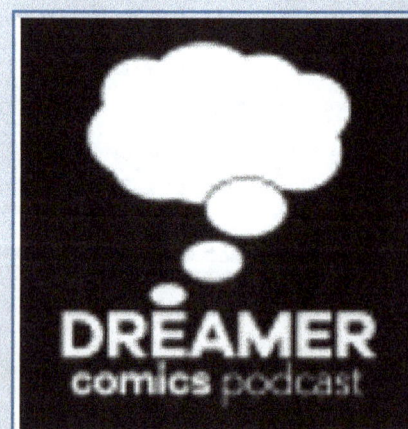

Medical Mixups

People get sick or injured all the time and seek medical care in a doctor's office or hospital emergency room setting. When story characters encounter these situations, realism will lend believability to the story, even in contemporary fantasy settings. Getting the details right keeps the reader engaged with the story and turning the page.

YOU CAN'T SHOCK A FLATLINE

When checking with medical professionals at all levels, the single fact most authors get wrong revolves around when to shock or defibrillate a patient to reset the heart into a correct rhythm. It's considered the most cringeworthy moment of medical mistakes in a book. Asystole (ay-sis'-toll-ee) is the medical term for a flatline on a heart monitor. The flatline means there is no electrical activity in the heart. This person is dead. Shocking them will do nothing unless your doctor's last name is Frankenstein.

If you want to shock a person after they go into cardiac arrest (let's call it "almost dead"), the correct rhythm most often seen on the screen is called ventricular fibrillation (VF). When VF occurs, a medical professional will administer shocks to defibrillate the patient and reset the rhythm to a normal heartbeat.

Also, no one uses the paddles you often see in movies and TV shows anymore. There are now two large rectangular sticky pads about the size of your hand. These are placed on the chest to administer the shock. The paddles started phasing out of use in the late 1980s, which is why it's so anachronistic when seen in stories occurring in the twenty-first century. To learn more about this, take a CPR class. You'll learn some life-saving training, and you can pick your instructor's brain after the class is over.

NO BELTS AS TOURNIQUETS

Another common mistake occurs when the hero slips off their leather belt to apply as a tourniquet to stop bleeding in an arm or a leg. A properly applied tourniquet needs to be incredibly tight. This is accomplished by using a stick or screwdriver as a windlass to twist the tourniquet material in order to tighten it to the correct pressure. Imagine trying to twist a one-inch sturdy leather belt in this way.

Instead, use the fancy silk tie your hero wears or tear the sleeve from a long-sleeved shirt to fashion a tourniquet. Many first responders now carry a small, commercially available pocket tourniquet to use when needed. You can buy them, too, directly online. If your hero is an action-type, consider having them keep one in their glove box.

YOU WON'T HAVE TO AMPUTATE

Contrary to popular belief, applying a tourniquet doesn't mean the person will lose their arm or leg. A tourniquet can be left in place to control bleeding for up to eight hours. This leaves plenty of time for a trauma team to begin surgical repair of the bleeding

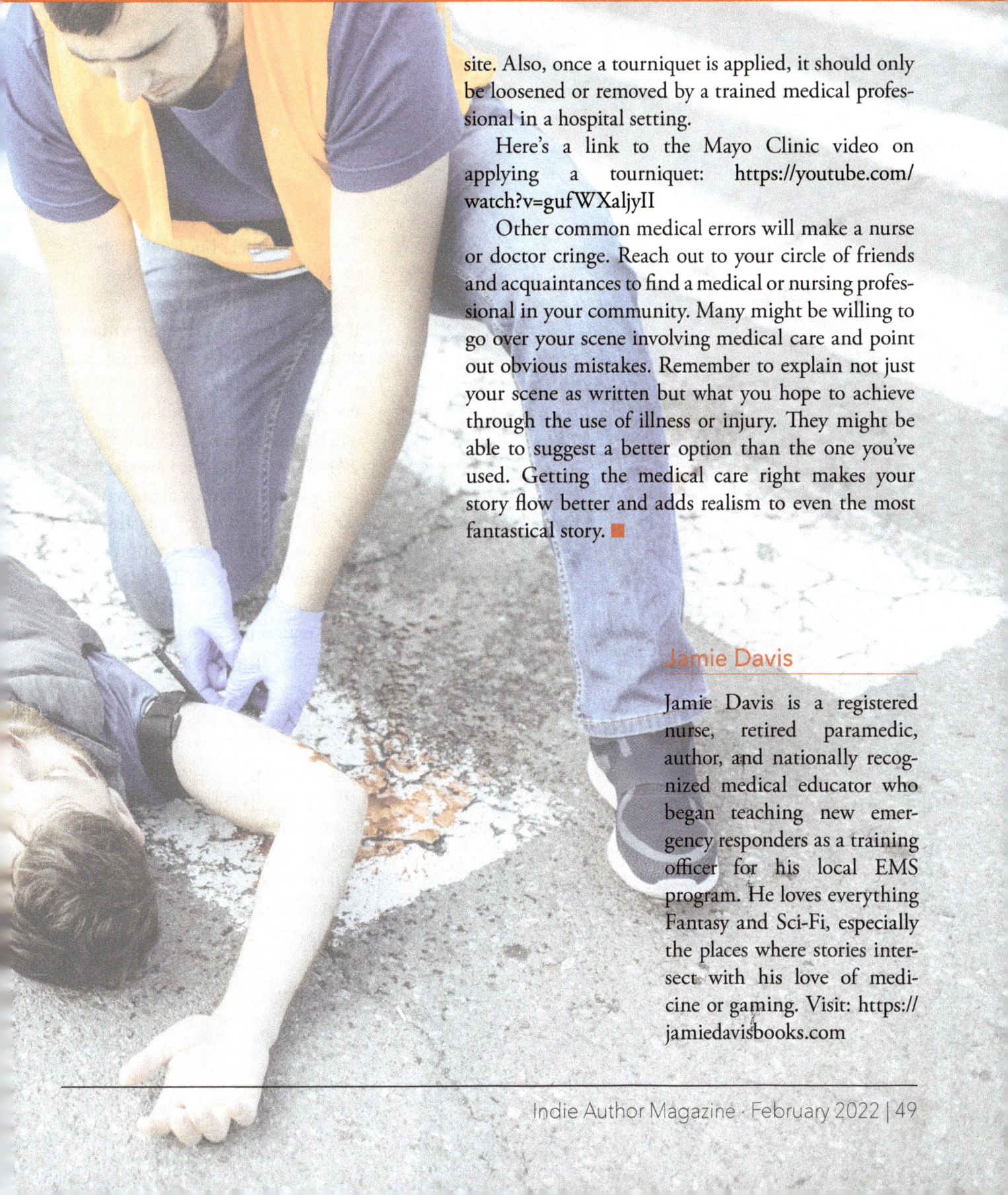

site. Also, once a tourniquet is applied, it should only be loosened or removed by a trained medical professional in a hospital setting.

Here's a link to the Mayo Clinic video on applying a tourniquet: https://youtube.com/watch?v=gufWXaljyII

Other common medical errors will make a nurse or doctor cringe. Reach out to your circle of friends and acquaintances to find a medical or nursing professional in your community. Many might be willing to go over your scene involving medical care and point out obvious mistakes. Remember to explain not just your scene as written but what you hope to achieve through the use of illness or injury. They might be able to suggest a better option than the one you've used. Getting the medical care right makes your story flow better and adds realism to even the most fantastical story. ■

Jamie Davis

Jamie Davis is a registered nurse, retired paramedic, author, and nationally recognized medical educator who began teaching new emergency responders as a training officer for his local EMS program. He loves everything Fantasy and Sci-Fi, especially the places where stories intersect with his love of medicine or gaming. Visit: https://jamiedavisbooks.com

Get Cozy

In her book *Writing the Cozy Mystery*, Nancy J. Cohen defines a Cozy as a "whodunit featuring an amateur sleuth, a distinctive setting and a limited number of suspects ..." When challenged, many authors will simply respond, "Think *Murder She Wrote* or Agatha Christie."

Simply, a crime occurs within a small community of colorful characters, each one with a motive and potential access to the victim. The viewer/reader unravels the clues in real time with the detective/ sleuth, dismissing red herrings until the final aha! moment when the perpetrator's revealed.

While a Cozy can be fast-paced, it is not a thriller. It is more of a puzzle, where the reader "pits themselves against the author to figure out whodunit before the murderer is revealed" as Sara Rosett says. Graphic scenes or references to sex, violence, and gore are inappropriate and will upset your readers as much as holding back on vital clues until the final reveal—the worst crime imaginable.

with Cozy Mysteries

Consider a traditional mystery story like a crossword or jigsaw puzzle. It's something to curl up with on a Sunday afternoon in front of a log fire or sitting under a parasol on the beach.

Mysteries are cerebral exercises based on unraveling relationships, whispered conversations, and timely observations. For cozies, these usually happen in an escapist setting, i.e., many take place in country manors, coastal towns, or remote villages.

Readers expect a further particular subset of tropes and themes from cozies. Nina Harrington lists the following ten elements as essential in a modern, Cozy Mystery:

1. Humor
2. Family-friendly content
3. An interesting setting or situation
4. An interesting story theme

   - Animals
   - Crafts and hobbies
   - Culinary
   - Historical settings
   - Paranormal and supernatural

5. A compelling and different story hook
6. A complete murder mystery puzzle
7. An amateur sleuth
8. A well-motivated murderer who is a match for the sleuth
9. Quirky sidekicks, friends, and family
10. Authenticity (i.e., you have to feel the writer loves the genre and is enjoying the story as much as the reader)

As most Cozies deal with the gruesome act of murder, they may not shy away from the deep psychological motives behind these heinous crimes, *but* they do not dwell there. Cozies are feel-good adventures where justice reigns and the sleuth always outsmarts the killer. Life returns to normal, and the sun shines once more.

Look at the most popular themes: animals, hobbies, and crafts, etc. Cozy murders take place in an otherwise idyllic world, a place where you would want to spend a vacation or retire. Their loving pet, quirky sidekick, supernatural partner, or paranormal gift often assists the detective in tracking down the clues.

Cozies are an increasingly popular and expanding subgenre of Mystery novels, whose roots lie with the traditional Mystery books of the Golden Age of crime. Cozies offer a way to escape from the horrors of the world. The Golden Age writers, such as Agatha Christie, were writing in the interwar years when their readers needed to escape and process their hopes and fears in a safe and comforting environment. Perhaps that is why Cozies continue to grow in popularity today. They often harken back to a nostalgic world in places populated with friendly neighbors, fun community activities, and beautiful scenery.

If you are thinking of writing a Cozy, bear in mind the five Ps:

- Puzzle
- People
- Place
- Plot
- Positivity

The outlook must be bright. Though we may have to suspend our disbelief that the local florist is better at solving crimes than the experienced detective inspector and wrestle with the legality of breaking into a locked cabin belonging to the primary murder suspect in the middle of the night, running throughout this nail-biting adventure is the knowledge that good will triumph, no matter how many hazardous or funny

> **If you are thinking of writing a Cozy, bear in mind the five Ps:**
>
> - Puzzle
> - People
> - Place
> - Plot
> - Positivity

incidents happen along the way.

You can have romance. You can have vampires. You can even have talking pets. But most essential of all, you must have a solid mystery with twists and turns, clues and red herrings, and a happy ending. ■

Susan Odev

RESOURCES:

Writing the cozy mystery–Nancy J Cohen

How to write a cozy mystery: the ultimate guide to writing modern cozy mysteries– Nina Harrington

How to outline a cozy mystery–Sara Rosett

Mystery: how to write traditional and cozy whodunits (Genre writer)–Paul Tomlinson

How to craft a killer cozy mystery: an intensive guide to traditional murder mysteries and writing the modern whodunit– Andrea J. Johnson

Standing and Walking Desks: Best Practices

Published in 2018 by the US Department of Health and Human Services, the second edition of the *Physical Activity Guidelines for Americans* suggests that adults should sit less and move more to experience "immediate and longer term benefits for how people feel, function, and sleep."

SIT LESS, MOVE MORE. THANK YOU, CAPTAIN OBVIOUS.

This isn't rocket science, nor is it new information. What is new in our aim for increased productivity is how we're incorporating movement into our lifestyles, including standing desks and treadmill desks, although their benefits probably aren't as significant as one might think. Surprisingly, using a standing desk burns only minimal added calories than sitting. And while treadmill desks can increase the opportunity for meeting activity guidelines, they're only effective if they're used as more than an expensive coat rack.

While they're not a magic fitness pill or even a caloric-burning boon, reports suggest they can still offer tangible benefits, such as lower blood pressure, improved circulation, better posture, and a faster return of blood sugar levels to normal after meals.

Roland Denzel, founder of https://IndestructibleAuthor.com and a restorative exercise specialist who works with

authors, offers a few observations and suggestions for those just starting out. He says one mistake that authors make is trying to stand too long or not changing positions often enough, leading to frustration and fatigue. He recommends changing things up with combinations of sitting and standing, aiming for at least five minutes of movement every thirty minutes.

He recommends leveraging the Pomodoro method many writers use to write in twenty or twenty-five minute sprints and using the five-minute break between sprints for movement. Once you've gotten used to it, you will eventually learn that it's possible to write more words in sprints with movement than you would in two hours uninterrupted.

MORE TIPS FROM THE TEAM

We asked a group of users for feedback and suggestions for those considering buying new equipment. We've edited their responses for clarity.

- Consider the surface on which you will stand. I found a padded floor mat increased my comfort standing for long periods.
- From working retail, I can vouch that your lower back is much more comfortable if you have the option to occasionally put one foot up on a ledge or block of some sort to change up your stance.
- I have a stand/sit desk and a wobble pad to stand on so I can shift between surfaces to eliminate fatigue. I'm a huge fan of being able to shift between standing and sitting. The option to change the surface you're standing on is huge too.
- If you have even the slightest issue with motion sickness, skip it.
- Just because you have a standing desk, doesn't mean you're better off. Pay attention to your posture and the ergonomics of your workspace. An improper keyboard/mouse/monitor placement will still wear you down.
- I have an adjustable height desk that I paired with this treadmill. The only thing I'll say is to make sure you have a way to turn it on and off easily in case you get phone calls. The treadmill isn't too loud, but the noise can still be distracting on the phone. Also, work yourself up in terms of time.
- I bought a standing desktop that you just set on top of your existing desk. It's a cheaper way to find out if you like them instead of investing hundreds of dollars in a product you might not use.

TRY BEFORE YOU BUY

If you're concerned about committing to a hefty price tag, one recurring suggestion from our respondents suggested starting small. Stack books on a sturdy surface and try it out for a week or two. If it works, then consider making the investment. You can determine if it fits with your lifestyle and fitness goals before shelling out big bucks.

WORK WITH WHAT YOU'VE GOT

Another suggestion is to purchase small modifications, such this height adjustable desk for your existing treadmill or this under-desk recumbent bike. Each is under $150 and doesn't require rearranging your workspace to test if they're a good fit.

Beyond the physical benefits, this article from Draft2Digital provides a more compelling reason to try out a standing desk: improved concentration and focus, which every writer certainly needs.

Whatever your motivation, with a little careful planning and some realistic expectations, the health benefits of using a standing or treadmill desk can make a profound difference for you.

(Thanks to Roland Denzel, Ashli Faron, Jamie Davis, Chris Miller, Chris Patterson, Heather Lynn Thompson, Jackie Dana, Marion Hermannsen, Kendrai Meeks, Christine Mecklenborg, Kimbra Swain, Paul Sating, Jen LaSalle, Rose Castro, Kasia Lasinska, Anne Marie Scott, Ivy Nelson, Deb Davies, Cedar Edwinloomis, Debbie Carver, and Tommy Landry for their suggestions.)

BONUS: Listen to the interview with Roland Denzel here. ▪

Chelle Honiker

PRIORITIZING YOUR WRITING

We can't escape it—we all lead busy lives, and we only have a finite amount of time and energy to fit everything in. It's little wonder our writing ends up getting pushed further and further down the to-do list. So how do we give it the priority it deserves in the time we have available?

BOOK A DEDICATED TIME

If at all possible, find some time during your day. Are you an early bird or a night owl? Carve out twenty or thirty minutes or any minutes for yourself. It doesn't have to be a daily slot, but book it regularly into your calendar make it a priority booking.

USE PROMPTS

If you're feeling a bit jaded when you sit down, challenge yourself with a prompt. You can find plenty on the internet or in books such as Julia Cameron's *The Artist's Way* or Monica Wood's *The Pocket Muse*. Keep a list of those that appeal to you to avoid the temptation of using social media.

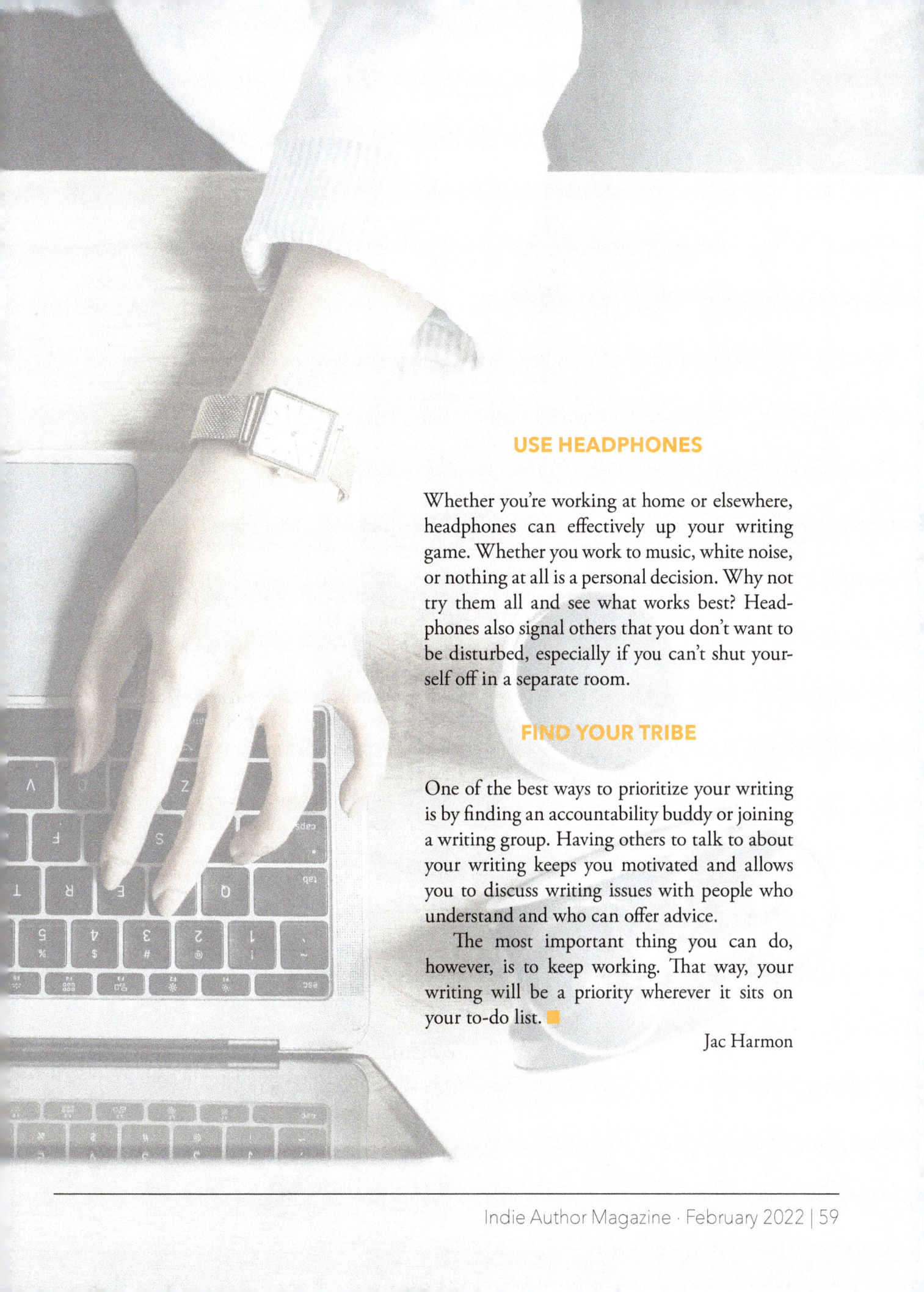

USE HEADPHONES

Whether you're working at home or elsewhere, headphones can effectively up your writing game. Whether you work to music, white noise, or nothing at all is a personal decision. Why not try them all and see what works best? Headphones also signal others that you don't want to be disturbed, especially if you can't shut yourself off in a separate room.

FIND YOUR TRIBE

One of the best ways to prioritize your writing is by finding an accountability buddy or joining a writing group. Having others to talk to about your writing keeps you motivated and allows you to discuss writing issues with people who understand and who can offer advice.

The most important thing you can do, however, is to keep working. That way, your writing will be a priority wherever it sits on your to-do list. ◼

Jac Harmon

Win the Short Race

THE KEY TO MARKETING NONFICTION

Say you're in a bar. With people. Someone approaches you and asks, "How's it going with your author business?"

You answer in one of the following three ways:

1. "Well, the CTR on my CTA is fourteen percent lower even though I increased my ad spend by ten percent. My unsubscribe rate increased eight percent, but worst of all, the fall-off rate increased at step four in my nurturing sequence, yet my ROI still increased four percent compared with last month. Hey, if I buy two drinks at the bar right now before the happy hour ends, we'll save fifty percent."

2. "Things are happening. People buy books occasionally. I might have made a profit last month, but I won't know until, well, I'm not sure because I don't really understand that part when they buy my books and then they are supposed to, well, do that next step, and something should probably happen. I could get us another drink if you'd like."

3. "I made more money than last month, and I know why. I already ordered us both another drink."

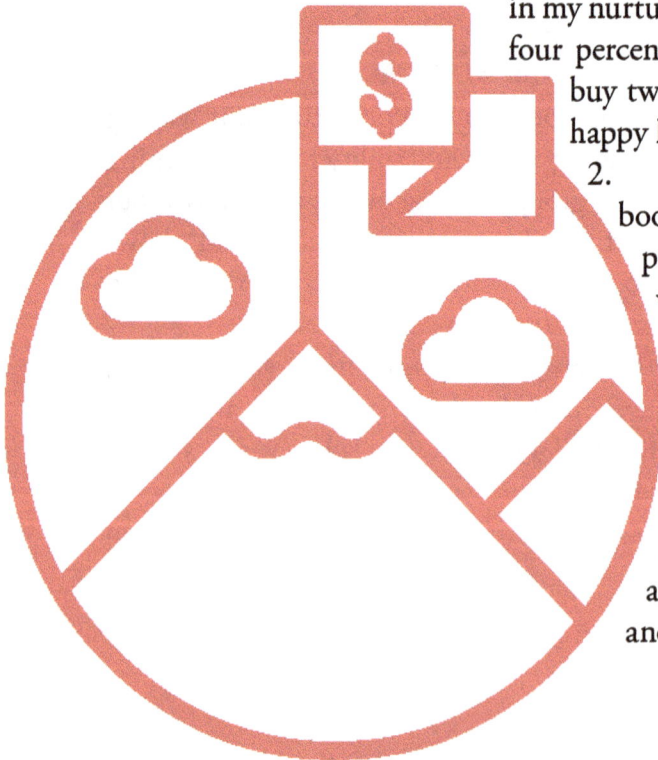

The "fast lane" is packed with traffic from everyone who thinks they have to do all of the things to become the nonfiction author superstar of their dreams.

Who are you?
Who would you like to be?

- Nonfiction Author #1 isn't human. Or at least is part robot/accountant/mathematician. Maybe part writer. Maybe 12 percent writer.
- Nonfiction Author #2 is probably having some success with writing. They probably enjoy writing. Hopefully.
- Nonfiction Author #3 has clarity and confidence.

Who was it you wanted to be again?

Certain authors we know (we won't name names) don't want to admit they're Nonfiction Author #2 but declare with passion they're in the fast lane toward becoming Nonfiction Author #1. However, that "fast lane" is packed with traffic from everyone who thinks they have to do all of the things to become the nonfiction author superstar of their dreams. Or is it their nightmares?

What if the dream were to become Nonfiction Author #3? The one who knows what's going on and what to do next and why and how to do it.

Did you catch that? It went by very quickly, and it didn't have any fancy marketing terms in it:

1. They know what's going on (clarity).
2. They know what to do next and how to do it (confidence).

If it seems a little like Author #3 knows what to do and has the confidence to execute, that's because that's exactly what's going on.

If you're reading this, thinking, *"Uh, yeah, a bit of clarity? Confidence in what to do next? I'd like that."* Here we go.

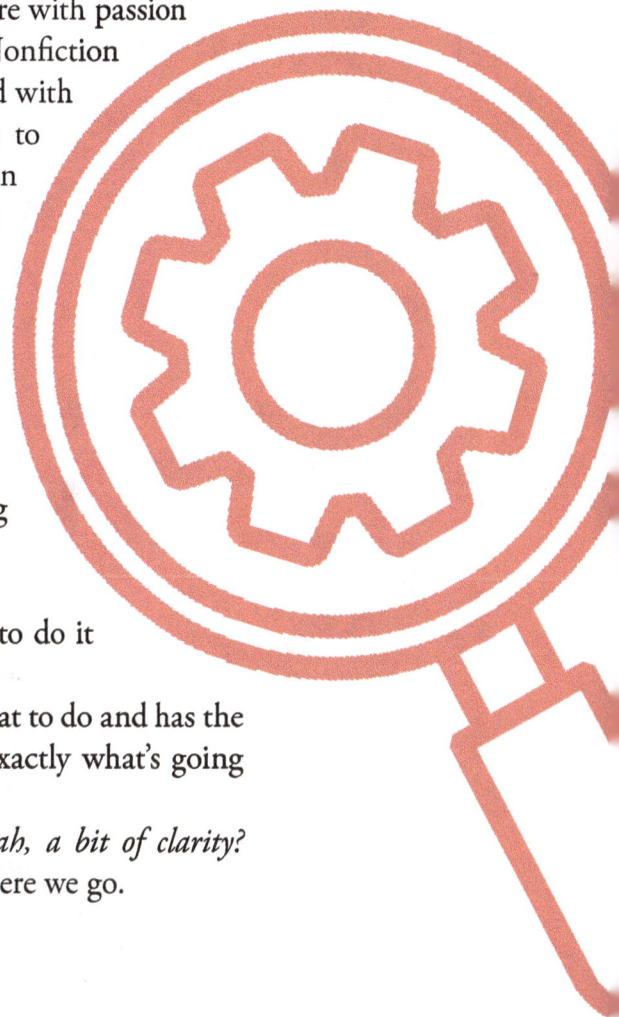

Even though a reader buys, possibly loves, and even hopefully reviews our books, we still don't know who that person is.

You will struggle to improve on a process that isn't finished. How do we know what's working and how well it's working if it's not actually working yet?

Pro Tip: We don't. We can't improve on something that doesn't exist. We need to first finish before we can improve.

What if we created the tiniest of processes, the simplest of roadmaps, the easiest of steps along a reader's journey?

Then we observed how it worked—or didn't. We saw what could be improved—and fixed it. We kept going with this tiny step until it was working well—before we moved onto the next step.

Does that sound simple?

It can be.

Do you know what's super fun about tiny assignments? They're doable. Do you know what happens when we finish things? We win. We succeed. We gain clarity and confidence.

On the other hand, what happens when we find ourselves down the long path of the slog, the never-ending traffic jam of the zillion things you're supposed to be doing on the road to somewhere, and you're not sure where you are, when you'll get there (if ever), or why you're even on this journey anyway?

Let's implement the tiniest of challenges to create a system that we can get working quickly. Ready?

1. Offer: Create a **link in your book** for the reader to get something from you.
2. Deliver: Set up a way for the **reader to get that item**.
3. Connect: Begin the conversation. **Track** who, how many, how often.

Notice there is no mention of technology, software, systems, or tools. We have all of the things accessible to us for free or low-cost.

Pro Tip: It costs five times as much effort, money, energy, time, etc. to obtain a new client as it does to retain an existing one.

Even though a reader buys, possibly loves, and even hopefully reviews our books, we still don't know who that person is.

Yet while that reader is in our book, while they have it in their hands, and while we're in their heads, unless they take an action and connect with us, the authors, they are still almost as hard to reach as another new reader.

Our goal, then, is to connect with that reader who wants to connect with us. How can we do that?

OFFER

The easiest way to think about an offer is to think about your mom. What would she want to know that's not in your book? If your mom brings up only images of homework and curfews, think of your biggest fan—even if imaginary.

What would they want to know beyond the book? In nonfiction, the ideas are only limited to your imagination—but also keep in mind what's relevant and enticing for them. It should also be easily consumable and doable for the reader (i.e., not another full-length book).

Some ideas are: video (you on camera adding to the topic), interviews (audio and/or video) of you talking with someone relevant to your book, a checklist (to help them keep track of what's in your book), or a roadmap. Deleted scenes are fun, even for nonfiction. Maybe a list of bad book title ideas.

See how this could be fun? Keep it light, easy, simple, and doable.

DELIVER

Without digging too deep into the technical aspects here, make an easy-to-spell link in your book (e.g. yourname.com/bonus) that leads to a landing page where readers can sign up to receive your free offer.

Keep this super simple. That landing page should have one hyper-focused goal: for the reader to enter their first name and email and then immediately receive your offer.

Any mailing list service worth its salt should make this possible. Set up a landing page and an auto-responder—an email that delivers the offer automatically after a reader signs up.

CONNECT

Entire books are written about this step, but many of us stop before we get there.

Pro Tip for Mindsets: Remember above about your mom? Or your superfan? This reader wants to hear from you. They read your book; they signed up for your offer. They like you. They want more of you. No, seriously.

Read the paragraph above three times, and then this email is easy to write.

In your mailing list software, you'll want to set up an auto-responder. What should you say? Thank them. Ask them how you can help or provide more for them. This is a crucial moment in your relationship with them, so use it strategically. Be friendly and be yourself. Keep it short, simple, and sweet.

What we want to achieve is this system, this roadmap, this—dare we use a marketing term?—funnel.

EVALUATE

What we want to achieve is this system, this roadmap, this—dare we use a marketing term?—funnel.

Get the simple thing done. Make it good. Make it better. Make it awesome. Are you wondering how to evaluate? The simplest thing to remember is not to compare yourself with others. Compare your funnel and numbers this month with last month, not the last hour with the previous.

Pro Tip: Have patience, and when you finish the tiniest of things, celebrate the win.

That's it. If you do this—complete this tiny task, test it, and improve on it—you're ahead of most in the "I just want to write the next book" camp of authors.

But get it done, because done is better than perfect—and so much more fun. ■

Bradley Charbonneau

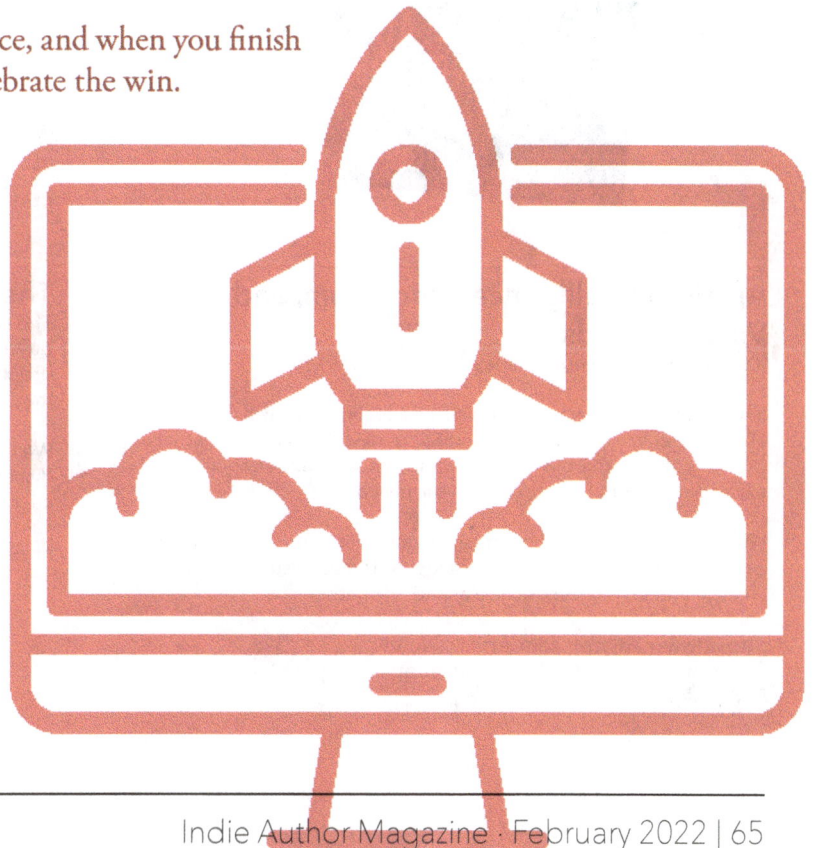

Books We Love

Courtesy of IndieAuthorTools.com
Got a book you love and want to share with us?
Submit a book at IndieAuthorTools.com

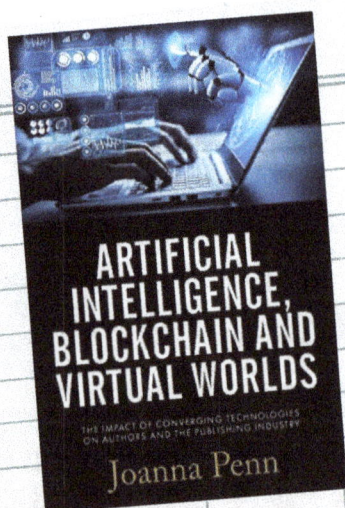

Artificial Intelligence, Blockchain, and Virtual Worlds

It's time to change our business model.

If we embrace this wave of converging technology, we can create abundance in our industry, enabling new forms of creativity, growing the market with new products and experiences, and expanding revenue for the entire supply chain.

We are creators. We turn ideas in our heads into books in the physical realm. We can use these technologies to surf the wave of change and invent the decade ahead — together.

https://www.amazon.com/Artificial-Intelligence-Blockchain-Virtual-Worlds-ebook/dp/B08P9S48D5/

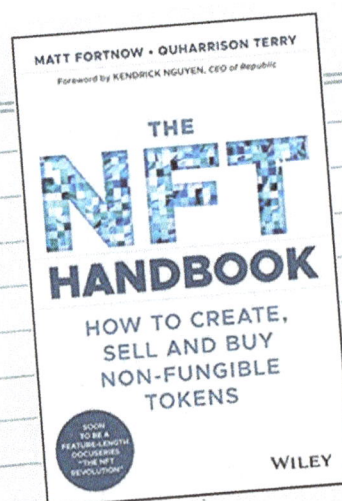

The NFT Handbook

The NFT Handbook is a detailed guide on how to create, sell and buy non-fungible tokens without the need for a technical background. Learn exactly what NFTs are, how they evolved, and why they have value.

We'll delve into the different types and aspects of NFTs and discuss the different NFT marketplaces and the pros and cons of each.

https://www.amazon.com/gp/product/B09FWQGP8K/

Audio For Authors

Audiobooks are the fastest-growing segment in publishing with double-digit growth in markets across the world. Podcasting has gone mainstream with listeners consuming audio on mobile phones and in-car devices, as well as through smart speakers. Advancements in voice technology continue to expand possibilities for audio creation and marketing.

With such rapid growth in opportunity, how can you position your books in an increasingly voice-first world?

https://www.amazon.com/Audio-Authors-Audiobooks-Podcasting-Technologies-ebook/dp/B0821PPC1X/

Audiobook Narrator

If you'd like to learn about audio book narrating from the performer's perspective, if you want an intimate, insider's look at how the industry's most acclaimed narrator approaches her craft...along with tips for anyone who records audio books, this is the book for you.

https://www.amazon.com/Audiobook-Narrator-Recording-Audio-Books-ebook/dp/

B00J131ESO/

How To Write a Children's Picture Book

Writing teacher and children's book author, Darcy Pattison (www.darcypattison.com/books) explains the craft of writing children's picture books. Why format matters, how to appeal to kids and parents, writing a read-aloud friendly book, and more. Tips on marketing your manuscript to publishers.

https://www.amazon.com/How-Write-Childrens-Picture-Book-ebook/dp/B0061OHCMS/

In This Issue

Executive Team

Chelle Honiker, Publisher

As the publisher of Indie Author Magazine, Chelle Honiker brings nearly three decades of startup, technology, training, and executive leadership experience to the role. She's a serial entrepreneur, founding and selling multiple successful companies including a training development company, travel agency, website design and hosting firm, a digital marketing consultancy, and a wedding planning firm. She's organized and curated multiple TEDx events and hired to assist other nonprofit organizations as a fractional executive, including The Travel Institute and The Freelance Association.

As a writer, speaker, and trainer she believes in the power of words and their ability to heal, inspire, incite, and motivate. Her greatest inspiration is her daughters, Kelsea and Cathryn, who tolerate her tendency to run away from home to play with her friends around the world for months at a time. It's said she could run a small country with just the contents of her backpack.

Alice Briggs, Creative Director

As the creative director of Indie Author Magazine, Alice Briggs utilizes her more than three decades of artistic exploration and expression, business startup adventures, and leadership skills. A serial entrepreneur, she has started several successful businesses. She brings her experience in creative direction, magazine layout and design, and graphic design in and outside of the indie author community to her role.

With a masters of science in Occupational Therapy, she has a broad skill set and uses it to assist others in achieving their desired goals. As a writer, teacher, healer, and artist, she loves to see people accomplish all they desire. She's excited to see how IAM will encourage many authors to succeed in whatever way they choose. She hopes to meet many of you in various places around the world once her passport is back in use.

Writers

Angela Archer

Having worked as a mental health nurse for many years, Angela combines her love of words with her love of human psychology to work as a copywriter in the UK. She independently published a novella and novel in 2020 and is currently fending off the lure of shiny new novel ideas to complete the second book in her sci-fi series.

When she's not tinkering with words, she's usually drinking tea, playing the saxophone (badly), or being mum and wife to her husband and two boys.

Bradley Charbonneau

Bradley Charbonneau wanted to be a writer. Trouble was, he didn't write. A friend was running a "Monthly Experiment" (no coffee for a month, wake up at 5 AM, etc.) and created one where everyone had to write every single day for 30 days. Bradley took the challenge. "Hmm, that wasn't so bad." Then he kept going. 100 days. 365. 1,000. 2,808 days and 31 books later and he found out it's simple. Not necessarily easy, but simple. #write #everysingleday

Jamie Davis

Jamie Davis is a registered nurse, retired paramedic, author, and nationally recognized medical educator who began teaching new emergency responders as a training officer for his local EMS program. He loves everything fantasy and sci-fi, especially the places where stories intersect with his love of medicine or gaming. https://jamiedavisbooks.com

Laurel Decher

There might be no frigate like a book, but publishing can feel like a voyage on the H.M.S. Surprise. There's always a twist and there's never a moment to lose.

Laurel's mission is to help you make the most of today's opportunities. She's a strategic problem-solver, tool collector, and co-inventor of the "you never know" theory of publishing.

As an epidemiologist, she studied factors that help babies and toddlers thrive. Now she writes books for children ages nine to twelve about finding more magic in life. She's a member of the Society for Children's Book Writers and Illustrators (SCBWI), has various advanced degrees, and a tendency to smuggle vegetables into storylines.

Gill Fernley

Gill Fernley writes fiction in several genres under different pen names, but what all of them have in common is humour and romance, because she can't resist a happy ending or a good laugh. She's also a freelance content writer and has been running her own business since 2013. Before that, she was a technical author and documentation manager for an engineering company and can describe to you more than you'd ever wish to know about airflow and filtration in downflow booths. Still awake? Wow, that's a first! Anyway, that experience taught her how to explain complex things in straightforward language and she hopes it will come in handy for writing articles for IAM. Outside of writing, she's a cake decorator, expert shoe hoarder, and is fluent in English, dry humour and procrastibaking.

Greg R. Fishbone

Greg R. Fishbone is an author of science fiction and mythic fantasy for young readers including the Galaxy Games series of middle grade novels and the mythic fantasy serial, *Becoming Hercules*. Greg is the founder of Mythoversal, a project dedicated to broadening representation in classical tales by amplifying historically marginalized identities and restoring traditions erased by centuries of gatekeeping. As a former Assistant Regional Advisor for the Society of Children's Book Writers and Illustrators, Greg co-directed regional conferences for authors and illustrators and presented workshops on a variety of craft and career development topics. He also served as president of the groundbreaking Class of 2k7 group of debut authors.

Jac Harmon

While studying for her doctorate in Medieval History Jac Harmon spent her time poking around in old buildings and reading manuscripts which gave her plenty of experience when it came to doing the research for her historical fiction. After many years spent working in university administration herding students she is now getting involved in voluntary work at a historic house and being trained in paper conservation. The idea behind this being that one day she'll be allowed to get her hands on some of the rare books in the library there. Not that this will help with her current novel which is set in the seedy criminal underworld of late-Victorian London. An era of gas lights and grime which was purposefully chosen to give her an excuse to indulge in her love of all things Gothic. Dark twists and bad weather are to be expected.

Marion Hermannsen

Marion is a bilingual author, working in both German and English. She holds a master of arts in English, Spanish, and Italian, as well as a diploma of marketing. She spent thirteen years both in London and Ireland while working in the finance and consulting industry.

Marion loves learning about writing craft and marketing best practices. She spends time mentoring other writers and enjoys the freedom of being able to work from anywhere.

She now lives in Frankfurt and is an active member of the local writing community, having published nine novels to date.

Her Irish husband has not only taught her the benefits of drinking copious amounts of black tea, but has impressed his Irish accent on her, to the amusement of her friends and colleagues.

Bre Lockhart

Armed with a degree in Communications and Public Relations, Bre Lockhart survived more than a decade in the corporate America trenches before jumping headfirst into writing urban fantasy and sci-fi, followed later by mystery under a second pen name. She's also one-third of a fiction editing team who probably enjoy their jobs a bit too much most days. As an experienced extrovert, Bre uses her questionable humor and red—sometimes other colors, too—glasses at writer conferences to draw unsuspecting introverts into her bubble of conversation; no one is safe. On her days off, you can find Bre camping and traveling with her family or organizing an expansive collection of lipstick at her home in Tulsa, Oklahoma.

Susan Odev

Susan has banked over three decades of work experience in the fields of personal and organizational development, being a freelance corporate trainer and consultant alongside holding down "real" jobs for over twenty-five years. Specializing in entrepreneurial mindsets, she has written several non-fiction business books, once gaining a coveted Amazon #1 best seller tag in business and entrepreneurship, an accolade she now strives to emulate with her fiction.

Currently working on her fifth novel, under a top secret pen name, the craft and marketing aspects of being a successful indie author equally fascinate and terrify her.

A lover of history with a criminal record collection, Susan lives in a retro orange and avocado world. Once described by a colleague as being an "onion," Susan has many layers, as have ogres (according to Shrek). She would like to think this makes her cool, her teenage children just think she's embarrassing.

Nicole Schroeder

Nicole is a storyteller at heart. A journalist, author, and editor from Columbia, Missouri, she delights in any opportunity to shape her own stories or help others do the same. Graduating with a bachelor's degree from the Missouri School of Journalism and minors in English and Spanish, she's worked as a copyeditor for a small-town newspaper and as an editor for a local arts and culture magazine. Her creative writing has been published in national literary magazines, and she's helped edit numerous fiction and nonfiction books, including a Holocaust survivor's memoir, alongside international independent publishers. When she's not at her writing desk, Nicole is usually in the saddle, cuddling her guinea pigs, or spending time with family. She loves any excuse to talk about Marvel movies and considers National Novel Writing Month its own holiday.

INDIE AUTHOR NEWS & EVENTS

For the latest on news and events pertinent to the indie author community, please check out our interactive calendar here:

Got news or events to share with the Indie Author Community? Let us know at news@indieauthormagazine.com.

Pssssst......

iAM 's First

AUTHOR
TECH
SUMMIT

May 11-13, 2022

Details to come:

AuthorTechSummit.com